The Grouch and the Tower and Other Sillies
by John O'Brien

Harper & Row, Publishers · New York, Hagerstown, San Francisco, London

To my parents

THE GROUCH AND THE TOWER AND OTHER SILLIES
Copyright © 1977 by John O'Brien
All rights reserved. No part of this book may be used or reproduced in any
manner whatsoever without written permission except in the case of brief
quotations embodied in critical articles and reviews. Printed in the United
States of America. For information address Harper & Row, Publishers, Inc.,
10 East 53rd Street, New York, N.Y. 10022. Published simultaneously in
Canada by Fitzhenry & Whiteside Limited, Toronto.

FIRST EDITION

Library of Congress Cataloging in Publication Data
O'Brien, John, 1953–
    The grouch and the tower and other sillies.

    SUMMARY: A collection of limericks, brief stories,
puns, and cartoons.
    1. Limericks—Juvenile literature.   2. Wit and
humor, Juvenile.   [1. Limericks.   2. Wit and humor]
I. Title.
PZ8. 7.O27Gr   811'.5'4   76-58730
ISBN 0-06-024601-4
ISBN 0-06-024602-2 lib. bdg.

All right, you can put 'em down now, but don't try anything.

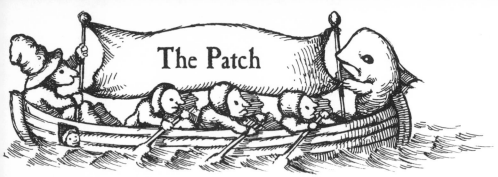

The Patch

The End

Some Limericks

A juggler from Paris, France
Had no clothes to go to the dance,
But since his beard grew
Half way to his shoe,
No one noticed that he had no pants.

Captain Scrub of the Robert E. Lee
Kept his boat as clean as could be.
He walked it on stilts,
So it wouldn't wilt
By touching the slimy green sea.

A dreamer who sat by the sea
Didn't budge for two months plus three.
But soon his left boot
Began to take root,
And grew into a ten-foot-tall tree.

An old man who shaved clean his head
Soon found that the sun made it red
But this silly fella
Would use no umbrella,
He went round with a shade tree instead.

A toucan who lived in Topeke
Found a crab for his supper last week.
When he went for a bite,
It put up such a fight,
That it gave him a very sore beak.

A musician with very poor vision
Picked up a sharp saw. Unwise decision!
It cut through the middle
Of his old bass fiddle
And himself with a perfect incision.

A nuthatch became quite a pest
When it grew too fat for its nest.
So it made up its bed
With the nest on its head,
Which made it a lark for the rest.

There once was a big-eared dragoon
Who had a collection of moons.
He tied them all down
When he went into town,
And sold them to kids as balloons.

A house that was built quite complete
Had everything including two feet.
It wouldn't stay down
On one plot of ground,
But jogged up and down the whole street.

The Grouch
and the Tower

A grouch lived in a tower.
A vine grew near by.

The vine grew toward the tower.
The grouch hated the vine,
and the tower hated the vine, too.

It began to grow around the tower bottom
and the grouch hated it more.
But the tower hated it a little less.

It grew farther up the tower
and the grouch hated it even more.
The tower hated it even less.

It grew even farther up the tower
and the grouch still hated it.
The tower began to like it a little.

It grew to the top of the tower
but the grouch still hated it.
The tower now liked it a lot.

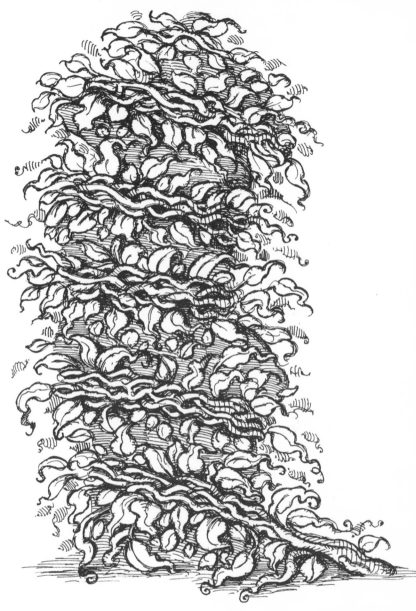

It grew over the top of the tower
and although the grouch still hated it,
the vine began to grow on him.

Soon they became attached.

The End

The Cloud

Some Puns

Got a dime? I'm short.

Spot, get off my tie!

But, your honor, he's lion.

Freeze a jolly good fellow.

Oh, wader!